Benjamin Banneker
Self-Made Man

Jody Jensen Shaffer, M.A.

Consultants

Katie Blomquist, M.Ed.
Fairfax County Public Schools

Nicholas Baker, Ed.D.
Supervisor of Curriculum and Instruction
Colonial School District, DE

Publishing Credits

Rachelle Cracchiolo, M.S.Ed., *Publisher*
Conni Medina, M.A.Ed., *Managing Editor*
Emily R. Smith, M.A.Ed., *Series Developer*
Diana Kenney, M.A.Ed., NBCT, *Content Director*
Johnson Nguyen, *Multimedia Designer*
Torrey Maloof, *Editor*

Image Credits: pp. 2-3, 24 Baltimore County Government; pp.4, 28, 29 NARA [535626]; pp.5, 6, 19. 29 Granger, NYC; p.8 Getty Images/ The Bridgeman Art Library; p.9 Courtesy of John Mahoney; pp.9, 15, 21, 29 Maryland Historical Society; p.13 Kim Karpeles / Alamy; p.14 Wikimedia Commons/Public Domain; p.15 LOC [LC-USZ62-58189]; p.17 (top)Internet Archive/Flickr.com/Public Domain, (bottom) LOC [g3850.ct000511]; p.21 From the African American Odyssey exhibit, Library of Congress; p.22 Rare Book and Special Collections Division. (3-13), Library of Congress; p.23 (top) LOC series: Series 1: General Correspondence. 1651-1827 Microfilm Reel: 014 , (bottom) U.S. Capitol/Public Domain; pp.25, 29, 32 Reference only image courtesy of Maryland Historical Society; p.25 Christopher Busta-Peck; p.26 Jason O. Watson / historical-markers.org / Alamy; p.27 Loop202/ Wikimedia Commons/CC BY-SA 3.0; all other images from iStock and/ or Shutterstock.

Library of Congress Cataloging-in-Publication Data

Names: Shaffer, Jody Jensen.
Title: Benjamin Banneker: self-made man / Jody Jensen Shaffer, M.A.
Other titles: Benjamin Banneker
Description: Huntington Beach, CA : Teacher Created Materials, 2017. | Audience: Grades 4 to 6.? | Includes index.
Identifiers: LCCN 2015051138 (print) | LCCN 2016000341 (ebook) | ISBN 9781493830824 (paperback) | ISBN 9781480756847 (eBook)
Subjects: LCSH: Banneker, Benjamin, 1731-1806--Juvenile literature. | Astronomers--United States--Biography--Juvenile literature. | Mathematicians--United States--Biography--Juvenile literature. | African
American scientists--Biography--Juvenile literature. | Scientists-- United
States--Biography--Juvenile literature. | Free African Americans--Biography--Juvenile literature.
Classification: LCC QB36.B22 S53 2017 (print) | LCC QB36.B22 (ebook) | DDC
520.92--dc23

LC record available at http://lccn.loc.gov/2015051138

Teacher Created Materials
5301 Oceanus Drive
Huntington Beach, CA 92649-1030
http://www.tcmpub.com
ISBN 978-1-4938-3082-4
© 2017 Teacher Created Materials, Inc.

Table of Contents

Self-Made Man

Benjamin Banneker was a free black man. This was rare for the time in which he lived. Back then, most African Americans were enslaved. Banneker was born free. He was also born curious. As a child, he loved to learn. He spent hours teaching himself how things worked. He studied why things happened. This inquisitiveness and thirst for knowledge continued throughout his adult life.

Banneker taught himself math and science. In his later years, he made up complex math puzzles for himself and others to solve. Banneker loved looking at the stars and planets. He liked to figure out their paths. His accuracy in calculating their distances later earned him an important job in Washington, DC.

Benjamin Banneker

Banneker was an author, too. He researched and wrote books. He also wrote important letters in which he spoke about the evils of slavery and **racism**.

Banneker wanted to show that African Americans were as smart as white people. That was something many people at the time did not believe. Banneker's achievements are impressive, even more so when one realizes that he achieved them with few resources and very little schooling. Banneker was a self-made man.

A slave trader sells a girl at an auction in 1780.

Slavery

In the 1700s, many African Americans were slaves. They were the property of others. Slave owners forced slaves to work long hours without pay. And they often treated slaves harshly.

Early Years

Banneker's grandmother was named Molly Welsh. She was a white woman from England. In 1683, she came to America as an **indentured servant**. Indentured servants worked for their masters for a period of time—usually seven years. In exchange, they earned their trip from England and a place to live in the American colonies.

When Molly finished her service, she bought a small farm in Baltimore County, Maryland. She began growing tobacco. Later, Molly bought two black slaves to help with the work. Eventually, she gave both men their freedom. Molly married one of the men. His name was Bannaka. Together, Molly and Bannaka had four children. The oldest was Mary.

A man sells a woman as an indenture servant.

It Was the Cow's Fault!

In England, Molly was a milkmaid, or servant. During milking one day, a cow kicked over a bucket of milk. Molly's boss thought she stole the milk. Molly was sent to the colonies as punishment.

When Mary grew up, she married Robert, a freed slave. Robert took Mary's last name. Their name changed over time to Banneker. Mary and Robert lived with her parents on the farm in Maryland. Benjamin Banneker was the couple's first child. He was born on November 9, 1731. He had three younger sisters. Banneker's parents worked hard. They saved their money. Once they saved enough, they bought 100 acres of their own farmland.

tobacco farm

Bannaka

Molly Welsh

Banneker's family tree

Robert

Mary Banneky

Benjamin Banneker

As a boy, Banneker helped on the farm. He cared for the crops, tended the horses and cattle, and kept bees. He also fished and hunted small game for food. Banneker's grandmother, Molly, took great interest in her young grandson. She taught him to read and write. Banneker read to his grandmother every Sunday from a Bible she had sent over from England.

When it was too cold to farm in the winter months, Banneker attended a one-room **Quaker** school nearby. Quakers believe in peaceful, simple living. They are against violence and slavery. Banneker attended school with both white and black children.

Quaker meeting

While other boys his age played outside, Banneker had his nose in a book. He absolutely loved to read. Banneker also had a gift for math. He liked to challenge himself with complex math problems.

Banneker didn't attend school for long. His family needed his help full time on the farm. But Banneker did not stop learning. At night, he kept his mind active by solving math problems. He also read any books he could get his hands on.

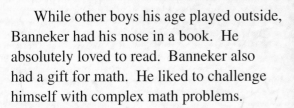

Banneker's notes

Bookworm

Banneker loved reading and books. But he owned very few. Some say that he was 32 years old when he bought his first book. It was a Bible.

Thinking Mechanically

As he grew older, Banneker became fascinated with **mechanics** and how machines worked. In his late teens, Banneker saw a pocket watch for the first time. Watches and clocks were not common in that part of the country. He marveled at how the watch worked. Banneker decided to build his own timepiece, or clock. He borrowed the watch, took it apart, and closely studied its moving parts. He made drawings of each piece. From the drawings, he calculated how much bigger he would need to make the teeth for the gears of a clock. He carved the wheels and mechanical works from wood. He added a few pieces of iron and brass, a dial, and a cover. Around 1752, after working for two years on his clock, he finished it.

pocket watch

Clocks and watches keep time using many intricate parts.

Banneker works on his clock.

Banneker's clock was so precise that it rang every hour on the hour for 50 years! It also made him somewhat of a local celebrity. Banneker became well known for miles around. People stopped to meet the young tobacco farmer and see his amazing clock. Then, in 1759, Banneker's father died. For the next 20 years, Banneker farmed and took care of his mother. But he never stopped studying and learning.

Two Timepieces

Would you believe that Banneker had seen only two timepieces in his life before he built his wooden clock? It's true! One was a sundial. The other was the pocket watch. Sundials rely on shadows and the position of the sun to tell time.

sundial

In 1772, change came to the area where Banneker lived. An **influential** Quaker family named Ellicott bought land next to the Banneker farm. They cleared the land for a flour mill and a general store. Banneker wondered if a flour mill could succeed. Most farmers in the area grew tobacco, not wheat.

Banneker became friends with the Ellicotts. He watched with fascination as the mill was built. When the mill was finished, he examined the big machines as they turned and ground the wheat. The mill and the store became popular gathering places for local people. A post office was even added to the land.

flour mill

general store

By this time, Banneker had become quite skilled at math. He created math puzzles and riddles for himself and others to solve. Many people knew about Banneker's talent. He was even asked to give his opinion on difficult math problems. **Scholars** from other parts of the country sent him problems to solve. Banneker gained respect from those he met. They found him to be intelligent, thoughtful, and kind.

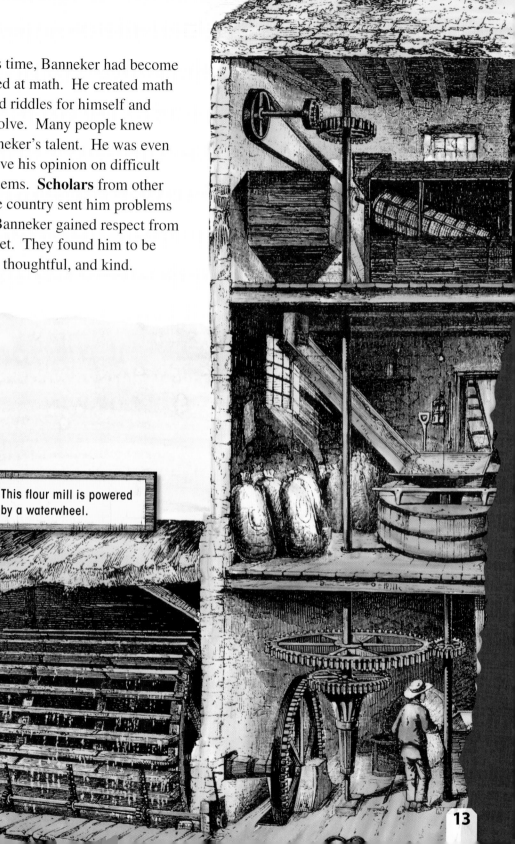

This flour mill is powered by a waterwheel.

Almanac Author

Banneker became very close friends with one of the Ellicott brothers. His name was George. The two men shared a love of **astronomy**. George let Banneker borrow his astronomy books and telescope. Banneker enjoyed studying the stars and planets. He spent many hours staring into the night sky. He even kept journals of his observations. George knew Banneker was good at math. He had an idea. Writing an **almanac** seemed like it would be a great use of Banneker's math skills and knowledge of astronomy.

1670 map of constellations

Banneker may have used a telescope like this one.

Almanacs are books that are printed every year. They are filled with useful and interesting information. They contain weather forecasts. They predict the best dates for planting and harvesting crops. They also foretell **eclipses**. They may include essays, poetry, sayings, and stories, too.

George encouraged Banneker to write an almanac. Writing a book of this kind is a big job. But Banneker was up to the challenge. He finished his manuscript in 1790 for a 1791 almanac. He sent it to three printers. But they took too long deciding whether to print it! It was too late to print a book for 1791.

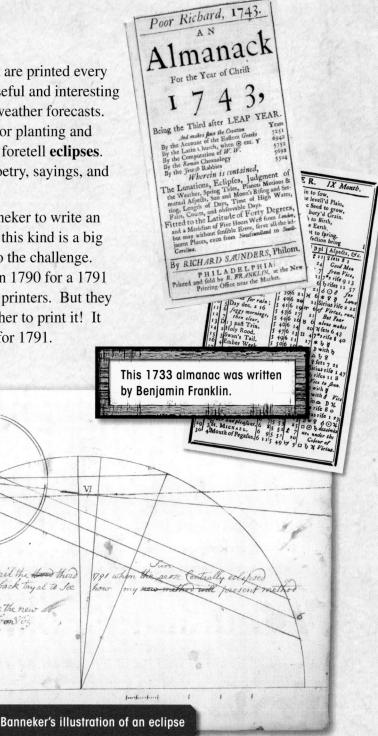

This 1733 almanac was written by Benjamin Franklin.

Banneker's illustration of an eclipse

Federal Territory

In early 1791, Banneker took part in a great adventure. He was asked to help **survey** the land for the nation's capital. Surveyors closely examine land. They take precise measurements to assess the land. This way, the land can be developed. Buildings can be built, and cities can be planned.

The land to be surveyed was called the Federal Territory. We know it today as Washington, DC. President George Washington chose the site. He selected a group of people to manage the project. First, a survey of the land needed to be done. At that time, surveying an area meant making charts of the stars from different areas on the land. By comparing angles, surveyors could figure out the distance between two points on the land.

surveying in the 1700s

George Ellicott's cousin, Andrew, was a professional surveyor. He was chosen to head the survey crew. Andrew needed a helper. He learned of Banneker's talents from George. Andrew thought Banneker would be perfect for the job of scientific assistant. At the time, Banneker was 59 and in poor health. But he took the job anyway. It was the first time Banneker had ever been away from home.

Andrew Ellicott

1793 plan for Washington, DC

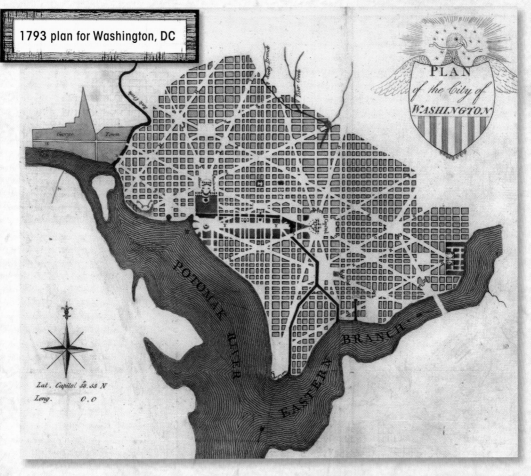

On the job in the Federal Territory, Banneker was tasked with watching the sky and checking the **astronomical clock**. Banneker had never worked with such an amazing instrument. An astronomical clock tells the time of day. It also gives information about the location of the sun and moon, the phase of the moon, and other details. Banneker's job was to check the clock's accuracy. He did this by looking at the sun and moon at regular times. He woke up many times during the night to record his findings. Then, he reported the data to Andrew Ellicott each morning. Banneker always made sure his calculations were correct. He was **meticulous**.

astronomical clock in Prague

One of a Kind

The most famous astronomical clock can be found in Prague (PRAHG) in the Czech (CHEK) Republic. It is over 600 years old. Tourists from all over the world visit the clock daily. It tracks the day, week, month, and year.

Banneker was the only African American on the job. The weather was cold and damp. The hours were irregular. He worked seven days a week. He had to live in a tent close to the project. But Banneker never gave up. He worked hard and finished his part of the job. Even though it was a valuable experience, Banneker was glad to return to his farm when the project was complete.

Banneker's surveyor's level

astronomical clocks

Letter to Thomas Jefferson

Back at home, Banneker began farming again. He also started work on a new almanac. He had learned a lot about the stars and planets while working in the Federal Territory. He applied this knowledge to his almanac. In June of 1791, Banneker finished writing an almanac for 1792. He sent the book to the printers. This time they printed it!

One of the printers was an **abolitionist** group. They were from Pennsylvania. They were against slavery. They believed all people should be equal. George Ellicott's brother, Elias, was part of that group. Elias saw Banneker's book as a way to show that African Americans were as smart as white people. The book sold well. Banneker soon became a household name. Travelers started stopping by his home to meet him. He showed them his clock while they were there. He was always kind and courteous to those he met.

colonial printing press

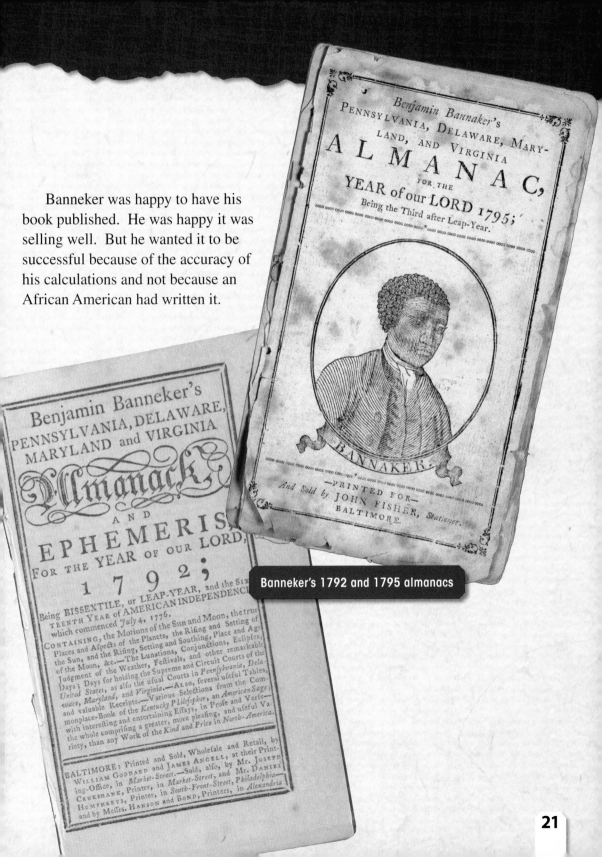

Banneker was happy to have his book published. He was happy it was selling well. But he wanted it to be successful because of the accuracy of his calculations and not because an African American had written it.

Benjamin Bannaker's PENNSYLVANIA, DELAWARE, MARY-LAND, AND VIRGINIA ALMANAC, FOR THE YEAR of our LORD 1795; Being the Third after Leap-Year.

BANNAKER.

—PRINTED FOR—
And Sold by JOHN FISHER, Stationer.
BALTIMORE.

Benjamin Bannaker's PENNSYLVANIA, DELAWARE, MARYLAND and VIRGINIA Almanack AND EPHEMERIS, FOR THE YEAR OF OUR LORD, 1 7 9 2;

Being BISSEXTILE, or LEAP-YEAR, and the SIX-TEENTH YEAR of AMERICAN INDEPENDENCE, which commenced July 4, 1776.

CONTAINING, the Motions of the Sun and Moon, the true Places and Aspects of the Planets, the Rising and Setting of the Sun, and the Rising, Setting and Southing, Place and Age of the Moon, &c.—The Lunations, Conjunctions, Eclipses, Judgment of the Weather, Festivals, and other remarkable Days; Days for holding the Supreme and Circuit Courts of the United States, as also the usual Courts in Pennsylvania, Dela-ware, Maryland, and Virginia.—ALSO, several useful Tables, and valuable Receipts.—Various Selections from the Com-monplace-Book of the Kentucky Philosopher, an American Sage; with interesting and entertaining Essays, in Prose and Verse—the whole comprising a greater, more pleasing, and useful Va-riety, than any Work of the Kind and Price in North-America.

BALTIMORE: Printed and Sold, Wholesale and Retail, by WILLIAM GODDARD and JAMES ANGELL, at their Print-ing-Office, in Market-Street.—Sold, also, by Mr. JOSEPH CRUKSHANK, Printer, in Market-Street, and Mr. DANIEL HUMPHREYS, Printer, in South-Front-Street, Philadelphia; and by Messrs. HANSON and BOND, Printers, in Alexandria.

Banneker's 1792 and 1795 almanacs

Banneker had strong beliefs. He was against slavery. And he wanted to prove that black people were as smart as white people. He also believed in the **Enlightenment**. It was a movement in which people said society would work better if it relied on reason rather than on emotion to make decisions.

A slave owner breaks apart a family by selling the father to another owner.

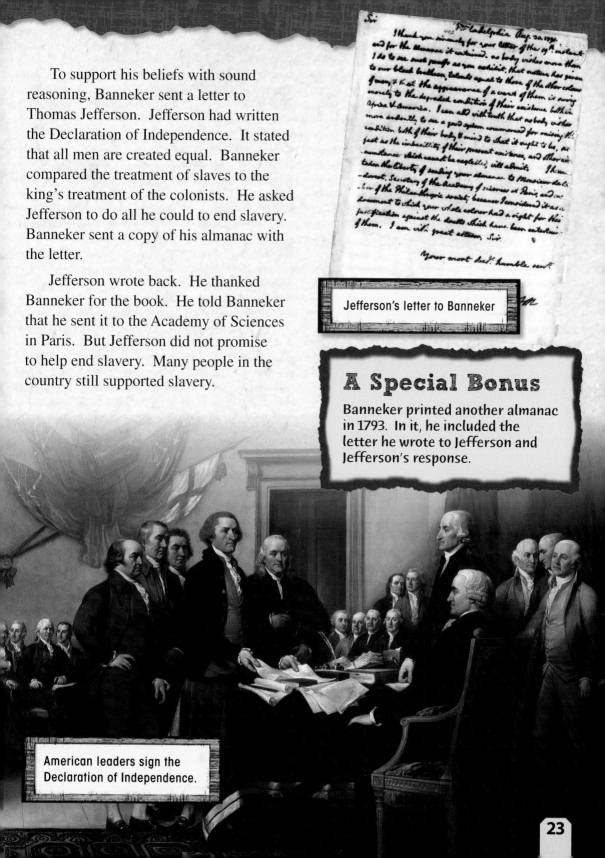

To support his beliefs with sound reasoning, Banneker sent a letter to Thomas Jefferson. Jefferson had written the Declaration of Independence. It stated that all men are created equal. Banneker compared the treatment of slaves to the king's treatment of the colonists. He asked Jefferson to do all he could to end slavery. Banneker sent a copy of his almanac with the letter.

Jefferson wrote back. He thanked Banneker for the book. He told Banneker that he sent it to the Academy of Sciences in Paris. But Jefferson did not promise to help end slavery. Many people in the country still supported slavery.

Jefferson's letter to Banneker

A Special Bonus

Banneker printed another almanac in 1793. In it, he included the letter he wrote to Jefferson and Jefferson's response.

American leaders sign the Declaration of Independence.

Final Years

Banneker continued to write and publish almanacs for six more years. The last one was published in 1797. But he had a hard time making enough money. He had achieved a lot in life despite racism in the country. Many people didn't want a free black man to find success. So he sold most of his farm to the Ellicotts. But he kept his cabin and a garden plot.

After 1797, life became more difficult for Banneker. He complained of headaches and bad health. But that did not stop him from living a full life. He spent much of his time writing essays and fantasies. He took walks on his land, and he gazed at the stars in the night sky. Banneker also visited the Ellicotts' store where he enjoyed talking with George about the government and current affairs. And of course, he still had fun creating and sharing complex math problems!

Crimes Against Banneker

In Banneker's later years, he was the victim of many crimes. His home was the target of gunshots. It was also broken into at least one time. Once, some boys stripped his trees clean of all the fruit.

replica of Banneker's home

On October 9, 1806, Banneker died at his home. He was laid to rest at the family burial ground nearby. On the day of Banneker's funeral, a fire burned his home to the ground. Nothing was saved of Banneker's work, not even his famous clock. Some believe the fire was **arson**.

On Sunday, the 9th instant, departed this life at his residence in Baltimore county, in the 73d year of his age, Mr. BENJAMIN BANNEKER, a black man, and immediate descendant of an African father. He was well known in his neighborhood for his quiet and peaceable demeanor, and among scientific men as an astronomer and mathematician. In early life he was instructed in the most common rules of arithmetic, and thereafter, with the assistance of different authors, he was enabled to acquire a perfect knowledge of all the higher branches of learning. Mr. B was the calculator of several almanics which were published in this, as well as some of the neighboring states, and although of late years none of his almanacs were published, yet he never failed to calculate one every year, and left them among his papers, prefering solitude to mixing with society, and devoted the greatest part of his time in reading and contemplation, and to no books was he more attached than the scriptures. At his decease he bequeathed all his astronomical and philosophical books and paper to a friend.

Mr. Banneker is a prominent instance to prove that a descendant of Africa is susceptible of as great mental improvement and deep knowledge into the mysteries of nature as that of any other nation.

Banneker's obituary

BENJAMIN BANNEKER 1731 — 1806 SCIENTIST

This plaque commemorates Banneker's life.

Solid Legacy

Banneker lived at a time in American history when most African Americans were bought and sold like property. They had no rights. They had no freedom. They were considered inferior to white people. Banneker wanted society to change. He challenged white people to see African Americans in a new light. He fought for equality.

Banneker's hard work as a farmer allowed him to take care of his family. His thirst for knowledge drove him to educate himself in math and astronomy. He was the first African American to publish scientific books. Common people, scientists, and statesmen all praised his work. His thoughtful and kind behavior gained him respect from those who met him.

Benjamin Banneker Institute in Philadelphia, Pennsylvania

BENJAMIN BANNEKER INSTITUTE

Founded here in 1854 and dedicated to the literary betterment of African Americans, this school was named for a Black astronomer and mathematician who published an al- manac and helped sur- vey Washington, D.C.

PENNSYLVANIA HISTORICAL AND MUSEUM COMMISSION 1991

Benjamin Banneker

This 1980 stamp was printed to honor Banneker.

Banneker later used his knowledge of astronomy to help survey the site of the U.S. capital. He was part of a team of men that placed boundary stones in the Federal Territory. Those stones mark the 10-square mile piece of land. They remain in the same spots. Like those stones, Banneker's **legacy** still stands strong. In 1980, the U.S. Post Office issued a stamp in his honor. It was a small tribute to a great self-made man.

one of the original boundary stones

BENJAMIN BANNEKER: SW-9
INTERMEDIATE BOUNDARY STONE
HAS BEEN DESIGNATED A

NATIONAL
HISTORIC LANDMARK

THIS SITE POSSESSES NATIONAL SIGNIFICANCE
IN COMMEMORATING THE HISTORY OF THE
UNITED STATES OF AMERICA

1980
HERITAGE CONSERVATION AND RECREATION SERVICE
UNITED STATES DEPARTMENT OF THE INTERIOR

Scrapbook It!

Think about Benjamin Banneker's life and his many accomplishments. Use the information you learned to create a scrapbook page about Banneker. A scrapbook shows the highlights of an event or a person's life. Print and cut out pictures related to his life. Paste them onto your page. Write a caption for each picture. Then, give your page a title. Make your page colorful and engaging. Below are some supplies you may wish to use.

- construction paper
- fabric
- glue
- magazine or newspaper clippings
- markers
- pictures of Banneker
- primary sources about Banneker
- scissors
- stickers
- yarn

Glossary

abolitionist—a person who wants to abolish or stop slavery

almanac—a book published each year that contains a calendar, facts about the movements of the moon and sun, changes in the tides, and information of general interest

arson—the illegal burning of a building or other property

astronomical clock—a precise clock used to time the movements of stars, planets, and other objects in space

astronomy—the scientific study of stars, planets, and other objects in outer space

eclipses—the partial or total hiding of stars, planets, or moons by the shadows of other passing celestial objects

Enlightenment—a movement of the 18th century that stressed the belief that logic and science give people more knowledge and understanding than tradition and religion

indentured servant—someone who works for others to earn his or her freedom or property

influential—having the power to cause change

legacy—something that happened in the past that will help the future

mechanics—science that deals with physical energy and forces and their effect on objects; the details about how something is done or works

meticulous—very careful about doing something in an extremely accurate and exact way

Quaker—a member of a Christian religious group whose members dress simply, are against violence, and have meetings without a special ceremony

racism—the belief that some races of people are better than others

scholars—people who study a subject for a long time and know a lot about it

survey—to measure and examine an area of land

Index

On Sunday, the 9th instant, departed this life at his residence in Baltimore county, in the 73d year of his age, Mr. BENJAMIN BANNEKER, a black man, and immediate descendant of an African father. He was well known in his neighborhood for his quiet and peaceable demeanor, and among scientific men as an astronomer and mathematician. In early life he was instructed in the most common rules of arithmetic, and thereafter, with the assistance of different authors, he was enabled to acquire a perfect knowledge of all the higher branches of learning. Mr. B was the calculator of several almanics which were published in this, as well as some of the neighboring states, and although of late years none of his almanacs were published, yet he never failed to calculate one every year, and left them among his papers, prefering solitude to mixing with society, and devoted the greatest part of his time in reading and contemplation, and to no books was he more attached than the scriptures. At his decease he bequeathed all his astronomical and philosophical books and paper to a friend.

Mr. Banneker is a prominent instance to prove that a descendant of Africa is susceptible of as great mental improvement and deep knowledge into the mysteries of nature as that of any other nation.

Banneker's Obituary

Obituaries are written about a person who has recently died. They are often printed in newspapers. They usually discuss a person's achievements or explain why that person will be missed. Read Benjamin Banneker's obituary. How did people in his time remember him? Then, write a new obituary for Banneker.